The Lightbulb Club

Starring…Essie, the Dog Who Learns
Self-Control

by
Sherry Hall

Sherry Hall

2

Table of Contents

The Lightbulb Club
Starring… Essie!
The Dog Who Learns Self-Control

The Lightbulb Club shows how to make the connection between elementary counseling programs and student achievement through the use of data. It puts counselors at the heart of student achievement supporting what is happening in the classroom while helping students maximize their potential with lifelong skills. It provides quantifiable relevance in the school reform effort and gives counselors a step by step way to support the Multi-Tiered System of Supports (MTSS) process by providing interventions to those students needing more than Tier 1 universal instruction.

While designed for the elementary level, The Lightbulb Club contributes to middle school achievement and high school graduation rates. It helps counselors use data to identify students experiencing roadblocks to success and provides early interventions in the child's educational career. Self-regulation is an important topic because of its correlation to the learning process and its connection to academic success, standardized test achievement, homework completion, and attendance. A strong foundation of self-regulation supports career and college readiness. This program blends self-regulation with brain science and promotes emotional intelligence skills with resilience, decision-making, anger management, and social skills.

The Lightbulb Club focuses on exercising the muscles of self-control and increasing learning stamina by sharpening mindful listening skills. It meets many state standards and American School Counseling Association (ASCA) Mindsets and Behaviors for Student Success: K-12 College- and Career- Readiness Standards for Every Student. It gives counselors a starting point in transforming traditional counseling programs into those that are data-driven and evidence-based. So with all of that being said, let's get started. It's time to meet Essie!

Essie, the Dog Who Learns Self-Control

Essie was a roly-poly puppy. He loved to have fun all the time but Essie needed to learn that when you go to school, there is a time to work and a time to play.

Essie was a student in Mr. Jim's First Grade. At home, he could talk whenever he wanted to but school had different rules. Mr. Jim would start teaching and something would pop into Essie's head. Without stopping to think whether or not this was a good time to for him to talk, he would shout out whatever he was thinking about, talking at the same time as Mr. Jim.

With more than one voice talking at the same time, it became a jumbled mess for all the others to hear. "Did Mr. Jim say to eat our math and do our snack?" said one. "No, it

was turn in our snack and take the last bites of our math,"
said another. What!?!?

At other times, Mr. Jim would ask the class a question he
wanted them to think about first before answering out loud.
Essie immediately waved his leg wildly, shouting "Ooh!
Ooh! Ooh!" and then blurted out the answer before it was
time and without being called upon. Nobody got to think
during "think time" because Essie didn't control himself.
The others then thought the only way they would get a turn
to answer is if they did what Essie was doing. Essie wasn't
setting the right example. The classroom sounded like a
noisy dog park and Mr. Jim looked like he was getting a
headache.

Rule #1: Show self-control by raising your hand and waiting until you are called upon. Put your finger over your lips while you wait if you need to remind yourself.

After lunch, Mr. Jim let the students choose a book and find a comfy spot in the classroom to read to themselves. Bob Boxer had found a cozy spot on the carpet and was just getting to the best part in his book when he noticed out the corner of his eye that Essie was "swimming" on the rug. He was inching closer and closer on his stomach getting into Bob's personal space as he was pretending to doggie paddle. No one knew why he was doing it but it interrupted Bob's reading. Instead of Bob's eyes on the words in his book, now he was looking at Essie. "Who swims on a rug?" Bob thought to himself.

Rule #2: Everyone has an imaginary bubble around them. This is their personal space. Stay in your own personal space and be respectful of others who are following directions. Show self-control with your body.

It was time for Art and the Art teacher, Mrs. Poodle, told the class they would be painting. Essie didn't feel like painting. He really didn't like Art. Painting was too messy and his pictures didn't turn out the way he wanted them to. One time at his other school, he spilled a blue blob of paint on his paper. They were supposed to be painting a picture of a jungle and so Essie made the blue blob into a big bluebird. He thought he had been very creative and was proud of what he had done, but the Art teacher scolded him about it. Essie decided he didn't like Art class or painting after that.

He scooted under the art table, sat there, and began to hum his favorite song loudly while he was under there. Mrs. Poodle asked him politely to come out and join the class but this turned Essie's humming into a loud howl. The others couldn't think about painting with him howling or hear the soft music in the background that was meant to get everyone relaxed and feeling creative. Some even held their ears to block out the horrible noise.

The Head Dog had to be called and when she got there, Essie wouldn't come out from under the table. In fact, he went under farther to get away from her. The Head Dog called for the Assistant Head Dog and both of them had to pull Essie out by the paws. He continued to howl as they nudged him down the hall to the office because he wouldn't go on his own. He bothered every classroom he went by with all of his noise. No one could work with all the commotion. Back in the art room, the other dogs could hear the soft music now and get back to thinking about painting since Essie wasn't in the room to bother them.

Rule #3: Follow directions even when you would rather not. Show self-control with your body, your mouth, and your behavior. Be the example for others to follow.

After his timeout and a good talking to in the office, Essie was allowed to join the others in his classroom. He didn't have any of his schoolwork done. He had not been listening well enough all day to understand what he was supposed to do. So while the others worked, Essie looked around the room to see if he could find a bug and when he got tired of that, he rolled his pencil across the top of his desk over and over and over again making an annoying noise. Then he got the idea of chewing the eraser off of his pencil and tossed it in the air playing catch with himself. After that, he made a paper airplane out of one of his worksheets and sailed it across the room when the teacher wasn't looking. It still wasn't time for it to be his turn for reading with Mr. Jim so he took out some doggieball cards he brought from home and looked at those and asked a classmate nearby if she wanted to see them, too. She didn't because she was busy doing her work. Finally Essie put his head back as far as he could in a big stretch. His head was almost on the student's paper behind him. "Stop it, Essie!" the other student yelled out. It felt good to stretch his neck like that and it gave him something to do so he did it again and again and again. Finally the other student got up out of his seat and found someplace else away from Essie to do his work.

Rule # 4: Are you being obnoxious to get attention? If so, stop it! Students with self-control are in charge of their voices and their bodies.

Soon it was time to go to recess. As the class walked down the hall in a line, Essie waited until Mr. Jim was around the corner. Then he got out of the line, did a little doggie dance, got back in line, and then stopped all of a sudden for no reason so the students in back of him ran into each other. When he turned the corner and saw Mr. Jim, he looked up innocently as if to say, "I've been doing just exactly what I should be doing the whole time."

Rule # 5: Choose to be someone that can be trusted to show self-control even when a grownup is not watching you.

At recess, the class played a game of Meadowball. Essie thought he was the best player and the fastest runner in the school but Carter the Collie must have had a special lunch that day that gave him lots of energy. He and Essie got to the ball at the same time and Carter kicked it away from Essie. Carter ran after it with leaps and bounds and kept it away from Essie who was trying his hardest to get it away from Carter. Essie didn't like this and tried to trip Carter with his leg when he got close enough to him. Then he nipped Carter on the neck with his sharp tooth. Carter scored the winning goal but instead of being a good sport, Essie said naughty words that should not be heard coming from a puppy's mouth. He was sent to the office and he told the Head Dog that Carter made him lose his temper and the naughty words had accidentally tumbled out. The Head Dog said Essie would be visiting with the counselor to learn that the choices he makes are his responsibility and about better ways to handle his angry feelings before he pops his cork!

Rule #6: You are in charge of the words that come out of your mouth. Show self-control by thinking before you speak. Take responsibility for what you do and say.

The Head Dog put Essie in timeout in the office and asked him to think about his day. How would he be ready for 2nd grade if he continued to spend his 1st grade days like this? Essie had to agree he hadn't done much to get ready for the next grade that day. Can you help Essie remember what he did that kept him from having a good day? (See how many of these ideas the students can come up with.)

*He not only interrupted his own learning but everybody else's.

*He spent his time bothering others instead of doing what he was supposed to do.

*He didn't stay in his personal space. (He got into someone else's imaginary bubble).

*He tried to get attention by going about it the wrong way. (Demonstrate with magnets to show how he repelled the other students.)

*He said words he shouldn't.

*He showed poor sportsmanship.

*He refused to follow the Art teacher's directions.

*He didn't try his best.

Essie felt ashamed and decided right then and there that he was going to make some changes. Only *he* could fix his problem. His mom couldn't do it for him. His dad couldn't do it for him. His teacher couldn't do it for him. It was all up to Essie.

Essie talked about it with his counselor. She invited him to join one of her groups called "The Lightbulb Club". What do you think they came up with so Essie and his classmates will be able to learn?

*He will show more self-control.

*He will stop and think about the choices he makes before he does them.

*He will treat others the way he wants to be treated.

*He will try his very best.

Rule #7: Be a good example of self-control for others to follow.

Essie began to feel excited at the thought of the new dog in town that he was becoming! He couldn't wait to show off his new self-control. And do you know that Essie realized that this kind of new dog was the dog he was always meant to be? Even his name lets everyone know what he is all about. Essie, or SC for short, is the dog with self-control!

Questions and Activities to accompany "Essie, the Dog

with Self-Control"

The story may be used in segments with the group addressing one part of the story in each session.
Rule #1

After you read this section of the story, start the discussion with, "What classroom rules do you know?" [Even though it is a small group, enforce the expectations that you are teaching them about self-control such as raising their hand and waiting to be called upon.]

Which classroom rules have to do with self-control?

Why do you think self-control rules are an expectation?

What should the student do?

1. The teacher is teaching math and Bobby suddenly remembers about the baseball game he and his grandfather are going to next weekend. He is so excited and wants everybody to know about it right now.
2. The teacher is teaching reading and all of a sudden, Mary's stomach feels like it is doing somersaults. She is sure she is about to be sick.
3. During class, Sally has noticed that John is playing with things in his desk instead of listening to the

teacher. She thinks she needs to let the teacher know right now.

4. During class, Sally saw John playing with things in his desk and something must have been sharp. John is trying to hide that he is hurt but Sally sees a lot of blood coming from John's hand.

5. Tommy loves school and he wants to answer every question that the teacher asks the class. It must be the teacher doesn't see him raising his hand because he hasn't gotten a turn yet. He's thinking about just shouting out the next answer.

Students write a goal they think they need to work on to have better days at school. (See Supplementary Resources.)

Rule #2

Think about a time you were thinking very hard trying to do your work. Without mentioning any names, what behavior distracted you? Give each member of the group an opportunity to share.

Take a minute to reflect on your own behavior. What do you do to cause noise when the class is working?

Roleplay a student at work and someone else who is distracting the student. Discuss: Why do you think this happens?

Do you have ideas of how not to notice when someone is making noises or wanting your attention? Write about it. Student share their thoughts.

Rule #3

Fill in the blanks.
Examples:

Even though I really wanted to run, I followed directions instead and <u>walked from the bus to the school door.</u>
Even though I really wanted to leave my trash on the floor, I followed directions instead and <u>picked it up</u>.

Even though I really wanted to stay in the bathroom and play, I followed directions instead and

_____.

Even though I wanted to call out an answer to the teacher's question, I followed directions instead and

_____.

Even though I wanted to talk to my friend when the teacher was teaching, I followed directions instead and

_____.

Even though I wanted to move to another seat to be near my friend when the bus was moving, I followed directions instead and _____.

Even though I really wanted to play with the toys I brought from home when it wasn't sharing time, I followed directions instead and _____.

Even though I really don't like to play the recorder in music class, I followed directions instead and

_____.

Using the same format, have students create and write their own statements and ask a group member.

Rule #4

Use magnets to demonstrate how obnoxious behavior repels other children from wanting to be someone's friend. Decide if the following behavior would attract (cause others to want to be around someone) or repel (make someone wish that the person would go somewhere else).

1. Spitting
2. Talking while the teacher is talking making it difficult for others to focus
3. In your personal space touching your hair
4. Showing you a toy from one's pocket during instruction
5. Telling a secret about another classmate

6. Velcro-ing and un-velcro-ing their shoe over and over again
7. Crawling around under the tables and desks
8. Yelling and then pouting because they weren't first in line
9. Everyone doing their part in a learning group
10. Asking you to give them the answers
11. Waiting patiently for their turn at the drinking fountain
12. Getting in your personal space wanting to hug you all the time

Read the song lyrics about Essie as a poem. Students will write their own poem about self-control.

Rule #5

Is this trust?

1. Mom and Dad can leave $5 on the kitchen table and they know it will be there when they come home from work.
2. Mom asks you to take care of your 2 year old brother while she makes a quick trip to the store. Your friends are outside playing football. Your little brother is watching TV so you go outside with your friends.
3. You begged to have a dog and said you would take it for walks every day before your parents got home from work. It's raining today and you don't want to get wet. Your parents will never find out.

4. You cleaned up the yard for the elderly woman who lives next door. She doesn't see very well and said she would pay you $10 but she pulled a $100 bill from her wallet instead. You told her she made a mistake by giving you too much money.
5. You're not interested in the lesson so you tell the teacher that you really, really, really have to use the bathroom. She lets you go so you don't have "an accident". When you get to the bathroom, you see kids from another classroom that you know and you join in splashing water on the floor, hitting each other with wadded up paper towels and flipping the light switch on and off.

Using words and drawings, students work in pairs to make a poster about self-control.

Rule #6

Draw a tic tac toe game on the board. Divide the group into 2 teams. Students take turns and decide whether something shows a good choice of what to do when they are feeling angry and ready to pop their cork. If it's not a good choice, what could they do instead to make it a good choice? If the student answers correctly, they can put an X or an O for their team. Play multiple rounds as time permits. Read the following:

1. Bobby was almost to the square that said, "Finish" and got the card that said to go back to the beginning

in a game of Candy Land. He folded his arms and pouted and said he wasn't going back.

2. Ted called another student a name at lunchtime because he didn't want him to sit next to him.

3. Billy dropped his lunch money when the class was lining up to go to the cafeteria. He had to find where his coins rolled to and pick them up and this caused him to be the last one in line. He pouted and cried about not being first.

4. Tommy brought his basketball to school to shoot some hoops at recess. He invited other students from his class to play, too.

5. Natalie brought a stuffed animal from home and had it hidden in her backpack. When the teacher was busy with a reading group, Natalie got up and opened her backpack to look at her toy. Another student saw her and told the teacher. Natalie hit the boy for telling.

6. When Charlie saw there was a substitute teacher, he didn't want to go into the classroom so he sat down in the middle of the hall. Charlie said he doesn't work for substitute teachers.

7. Martha wanted to sit by her friend at lunch but all the seats around her were taken. She found another place to sit and talked to those students instead.

8. There are only three computers in the classroom and Jack wanted to be at one of them. Since there was not one available, Jack sat down anyway and shoved Mike out of the seat.

9. Emily doesn't like music class so she refused to participate.

10. Keith's class was playing kickball at recess. Keith made a great kick and ran around the bases. Just as he got to home base, someone from the other team threw the ball and Keith was out but Keith didn't want to be out. He began pushing someone from the other team and arguing.
11. The boy behind Susie on the bus yelled in her ear so she got up out of her seat while the bus was moving and punched him.
12. When Bobby plays a certain game, he always gets the blue game piece. Someone else chose it before Bobby did so Bobby chose his next favorite color.

Students write about a time they showed self control with their anger and include how it made them feel to keep their cork in the bottle.

Rule #6

Think of a new goal related to school that you would like to make for yourself. Everyone has something to work on. What's yours?

Goal:_____

_____

_____

What will you have to do to make this come true? What do you have to do differently? What needs to improve? Write about it.

_____

_____

_____

_____

Essie and Sam Carter

Essie remembered what he learned about self-control. The shortcut way of writing his name (SC) was a reminder he kept with him all the time. He felt much happier now and had so many friends. He loved school!

Essie's cousin had visited him over the summer and he was really interesting to talk to. Essie had been learning about how his brain works. He found out that his amygdala tells him the first thing to think or feel, a reaction, but it's not always the best choice to make when solving a problem. Like when he's walking in line down the hall and the line stops all of a sudden and the dog behind him doesn't. Then the back of Essie's foot gets stepped on and it doesn't feel good. Essie used to react to his first feeling. He felt angry about it and was ready to fight about things like that. That was his amygdala talking. But now he stops and thinks before he acts. He knows the dog behind him didn't do it on purpose so when the dog apologizes, Essie just smiles and says, "No problem" instead of making a big deal out of it. He knows he makes mistakes, too.

Rule #1: Your amygdala is a reaction, the first feeling you have after something happens or the first thing you think of doing, but you need to stop and give your brain time to think, to see if it is the best choice you can come up with.

Essie noticed that one of his friends wasn't watching where he was going out at recess. He was fascinated watching a plane fly overhead. My friend thought that it was pretty cool the way it went in and out of the clouds. But when you're not watching where you're going, you're not being mindful. Your mind isn't full of right here, right now, and being aware of everything around you. My cousin told me all about mindfulness.

Anyway, my friend was going in one direction and a new dog, Sam Carter, was running in the other direction playing a game and they smacked into each other, quite by accident. Sam showed his teeth, growled, and said it had better never happen again, or else. He gave my friend such a scary look that it made my friend cry. It's true that my friend needed to be more mindful about what he was doing but Sam Carter didn't have to be so mean about it either. That's no way to make friends.

"There must be lots of dogs that need to learn about self-control," thought Essie. He could spot it right away because he was somewhat of an expert about self-control now.

Rule #2: When you are being mindful, that is, your mind is full of right here, right now, it can prevent a lot of problems from happening.

The next day in the cafeteria, one of my friends dropped his tray. The tray made an echo-y noise as it hit the floor and everyone turned to see what had just happened. We were having spaghetti and it went flying everywhere, even on top of my friend's head! What a mess. I noticed some dogs laughed and Sam Carter seemed to be laughing the loudest and pointing at my friend. He did look kind of funny and laughing was the first thing I thought of doing, too, but then I remembered the day I dropped my tray in first grade. My cousin told me that I am using another part of my brain when I remember things. It's called my hippocampus. It sounds a lot like hippopotamus but I know I don't have a hippo living inside my head! Anyhow, I remembered how embarrassed I felt when I dropped my tray and everyone was looking at me. Not one dog would even help me. So this time, I made the choice not to laugh. I got out of my seat, got some napkins and started helping my friend clean up the mess until the custodian came over with a mop. I told my friend not to worry about it. We all make mistakes and that is okay. My friend knew I was a *real* friend by the choice I made after I stopped and thought about it.

Rule # 3: Stop and give your brain a chance to do its best thinking. Your hippocampus is like the teacher's filing cabinet with information and memories you have saved.

Later that afternoon, I noticed in the classroom when the teacher was talking about math, that Sam Carter had brought some baseball cards from home and was looking at those instead. He was not on the teacher's channel. I remember our counselor visited our class one time and said we are in charge of our minds like a TV remote control. If the teacher is teaching on Channel 9, then we need to be tuned in to Channel 9, too. If we are on Channel 12, for example, where baseball card-looking is going on, we are missing the math lesson that's happening on Channel 9. We have to be mindful and have our minds full of what's going on right here, right now. When we notice our brain is drifting to a different place, we need to bring it back.

When a pilot puts a plane on autopilot, he is no longer flying the plane. He can be thinking about something else or might even get up and walk around. When the teacher is teaching, be sure you are not on autopilot. Your body and your thinking brain both need to be in the classroom. Make eye contact with the teacher. Look at his or her eyes. What color are they? See if you can repeat to yourself in your head what the teacher just said. What connection with something you know, can you make with what you just heard? Stick with it and if you catch yourself drifting off course again, pull yourself back and begin again by making eye contact.

Rule # 4: Practice training your brain to be right here, right now. Get off autopilot and be in control of where your thinking goes. If you are on a different channel, use your imaginary remote control and switch your mind back to where it belongs.

Because Sam's brain was on a different channel with the baseball cards, he had no idea how to do the math problems the teacher was just talking about. The teacher said, "Take out your math journal and show two ways you could solve the first problem." What page was she talking about? Where's my math journal? Where's my pencil? Question number one had nothing to do with baseball or the cards he had been looking at. Sam didn't know what to write. He looked around and realized he was the only dog who wasn't getting right to work. The teacher was on her over to Sam's desk when he began to cry big basset hound tears.

The teacher saw the baseball cards in Sam's desk and put them in the June Box. By now, everyone had stopped working on math and was looking at Sam. Not only had he distracted himself from learning, but now he was distracting others. The teacher told Sam that he made a mistake bringing the baseball cards to school. Toys, cards, and things that can distract our learning need to be left at home.

Then she said something really surprising! She said that

making mistakes can be a good thing. I was sure I hadn't

heard her right but then she explained. As long as we stop

and think after we make a mistake and come up with another

way, mistakes are okay. They help our brain stretch just like

a rubberband and that makes us better thinkers.

Rule #5: Mistakes can help us learn as long as we reflect
and think about what we can do differently the next
time. After hearing that and thinking about it, Sam
Carter came up with his own math problem:

Mistakes + Thinking Afterwards = Better Choices

Sam had discovered something important about mistakes

but maybe he didn't realize he could use it in other situations

and not just with his classroom subjects. It was time for PE and Sam wanted to be team captain and choose the dogs he wanted for his kickball team. The coach chose someone else to be the captain and Sam howled loudly about it. Sam and the coach went nose to nose. Sam had made another mistake and was being so disrespectful. My cousin would say that Sam needed to use his pre-frontal cortex or PFC to stop and think of a better choice before he did or said something he shouldn't. Our PFC is located right behind our forehead and makes all of our important, executive decisions. Sam could use his hippocampus to help him remember what happens next when someone is disrespectful to someone else, especially grown-ups. He could stop and think about what it means to be a good sport. Sam could also remember that at school, there are many dogs who need to have a turn. He can't always have things his way.

If Sam would have stopped to think, he could have shown some self-control by telling himself, "It's okay. Maybe next time I'll be the team captain." Then he could have joined a team and had some fun. It was too late for him to make the better choice this time. Instead he had to take a time-out against the wall and sit and watch everyone else play.

Rule # 6: Take time before you speak or act to give your pre-frontal cortex a chance to come up with the best choice. Think what might happen next if you say or do what you are thinking about. Is that what you want to happen? You are in control of the choices you make.

Essie noticed that Sam Carter was having the same problem Essie used to have with self-control. He had a chat with Sam about it after school and shared what his cousin had told him about how our brains work. Essie noticed that Sam started to take his time to think about better ways of handling his feelings. And if he did make a mistake, he stopped to think about what he could have done instead. Over time, Sam began to feel prouder of the choices he was making and the other dogs began to want him for a friend. Essie knew that Sam could do it. We already know that Essie or SC became a pro at self-control. And one day, Essie realized something pretty amazing! He couldn't wait to tell Sam what else he had discovered. He looked everywhere for him and finally found him at the dog park playing with some other dogs. He ran up to Sam all out of breath.

"Sam! Sam! Guess what I found out? You are an SC, too!" Can you figure out what Essie meant by that? (Pause for answers.)

Rule #7: Even if your initials aren't SC, you can still be a pro at self-control if you stop and think and give your brain a chance to make the best choice. Put all three parts of your brain to work. Think about what your amygdala is telling you but use your hippocampus and your pre-frontal cortex to help you make the best decision.

Questions and Activities to accompany "Essie and Sam Carter"

The story may be used in segments with the group addressing one part of the story in each session. Use "The Lightbulb Club Game" and "The Game of Self-Control" board games as time permits.

Rule #1

Your amygdala is the first thing your mind thinks of when something happens. It tries to keep you safe but not everything is a threat that you need to react to. Your amygdala might tell you to fight, run or freeze.

1. When would it be a good choice to listen to your amygdala if it told you to freeze? (a bee is buzzing around you)

2 Run? (get outside as quickly as you can if your house is on fire)

3. Fight? (a stranger is grabbing your arm)

Present the first stanza of the poem found in the Supplementary Resources section. If you can write it out on a whiteboard or write it on post-it poster paper, students will be able to read it. Have students repeat after you and then read aloud by themselves if grade level appropriate.

4. What does it mean "let me think a minute, please"? Why would you want to?

5. Add actions for fight (make fists), run (in place), freeze (like a statue), the first thing (put index finger in air) let me think (put fingers on side of head like you are thinking)

Say first stanza again with actions.

Rule #2

Mindfulness is thinking about what is going on all around you right here, right now, today. Have students get quiet, close their eyes and listen. After a minute, facilitator asks them to share what they heard in the quiet. If someone shares something that is happening somewhere else (e.g., my baby brother crying), explain that their mind went somewhere else other than right here, right now.

Discussion Questions: Mindfulness is thinking about right here, right now and it also is thinking about how our actions may affect others.

What might happen?

1. When someone is driving, they are looking at a text on their phone they just received.

2. Someone is next in line for the slide and since they're at he top of the ladder, it must be okay to slide down without looking at what's going on down below.

3. Someone spilled their milk on the cafeteria floor and a student is busy talking to a classmate and walks right through it.

4. Someone is walking down the street looking at their cell phone.

5. Someone doesn't realize their shoes are untied and they begin running at PE.

6. Someone is angry with someone else so they use their older sister's Facebook page to post something unkind.

7. Someone took the last treat in the box and left the empty box in the freezer.

8. Someone left their bedroom door open and the cat has been wanting to meet the hamster in the cage on the dresser.

To get students' minds quiet and focused on the right here, right now, teach mindful breathing (4 counts in and 4 counts out, giving a pinwheel to each to blow to keep the exhale going long enough).

You can also use a snowglobe or make your own mindfulness jar. Get a clear plastic container and use water, sand, baubles, shells, buttons, anything you can find to make it interesting. Shake it up and make the correlation that when we are stressed or upset or thinking about too many things at one time, it causes swirling thinking. It is difficult to get a clear picture of how problems should be solved.

Have the group watch quietly as everything settles to the bottom. Help students become mindful and aware of their breathing. Make the comparison to inner peace. When we are peaceful inside, we can do our best thinking.

Rule #3

Have students look around to see if there is a filing cabinet nearby. What do they suppose is inside? (things someone wants to keep, important papers) Our brain has a filing cabinet where everything they've learned or heard is stored called the hippocampus. It does a lot of its work when they are sleeping. Put in a plug for getting their "magic 10" hours of sleep every night---the amount of time their brain needs to sort and file things they need to remember and throw out the information they don't.

This is also where consequences of behavior are stored. Ask students to think about a time when they got off track with their behavior. What happened next? What was the consequence? How did they feel about their behavior choice? What did they learn?

Next time they need to make a choice about behavior, their hippocampus can help them remember what they learned in the past about a choice. They can use what they learned to help them make the best decision in the future.

Present the 2nd stanza of the poem. They repeat. Ask students to share one thing they have stored in their hippocampus.

Add actions: 1st line, they pretend they are pulling out a drawer in the filing cabinet.

"Everything", they make a large gesture using both hands to show "the whole".

Act out while reading the second stanza of the poem.

Rule #4

Bring a remote control from home and demonstrate how right here, right now is on one channel but sometimes boys and girls change the channel and go somewhere else in their minds. Where do they remember going? What have they noticed other students doing when their teacher is teaching? (No students name mentioned)

Explain that when they notice they are on a different channel, that they need to take control and get back in focus with right here, right now.

Review tips mentioned in the story.

Ask students to repeat what you just said.

Rule #5

Have students tell an "elbow partner" about a mistake they made and what they learned from it.

Demonstrate repeatedly running into the table because I was looking somewhere else, for example. That is not a helpful mistake because I didn't think after it happened and learning did not occur.

Then demonstrate running into the table, stopping and thinking about what I could do differently so it doesn't happen again, and then show walking around the table because now I am watching what I am doing.

Or

Wear two different-colored similar shoes for the group session and point out your mistake of not turning on the closet light to choose your shoes that morning. You are feeling embarrassed about it. When you thought about it, you learned that if you turn on the closet light when getting dressed, you will be able to see the color of your shoes and make a better choice.

Play Game: "Helpful or Not a Helpful Mistake" (Supplementary Resources section)

Reinforce Carter's equation about mistakes:

Mistakes + Thinking Afterwards = Better Choices

Designate two areas on a white board, or in two hula hoops on the floor, or two signs to stand behind. Read the scenarios and have individual students decide whether it was a mistake that was helpful or not helpful and explain their reasoning.

Rule #6

Teach last stanza of poem about the PFC.

What does it mean "Let me stop and think about a choice so good to shout about?"

What kinds of choices are we so proud of that we want other people to know?

Practice actions that go with the words:

Spell out P-F-C across their forehead with their finger.

Make a stop signal with hand on "let me stop".

Cup both hands together by mouth for "shout about".

Make heart sign for "love" and point to their head for the word "brain".

Recite entire poem with actions.

Present scenarios to get students thinking how all three parts of their brains work together.

Example: The doorbell rings and when they peek out the window by the door, they see two ghosts standing there!

What would their Amygdala tell them to do? (This is scary! Run or freeze- don't let them see you)

What would their Hippocampus remember? (It's October 31st)What would their PFC tell them to do? (Open the door and give them some candy)

Using the model, think about the following.

You are upstairs playing and you hear a loud noise. What do the three parts of your brain tell you?

Your brother borrowed your iPod and when he gave it back, it no longer worked.

You love to play basketball and you wanted to join a game going on at recess but one of the kids said they didn't want you to play.

Game: Which Part of the Brain? (Supplementary Resources section)

Students will identify the part of their brain that would be working with the scenarios presented.

Essie and Cherri Chihuahua

Essie looked forward to being in 3rd Grade. He was proud of it all summer. He would be taking the important state tests this year. How grown up is that?! He was sure glad that he had learned about self-control back when he was a 1st grader. He knew how to tune in to the teacher's channel, stay in his invisible bubble, and not be a distraction to other dogs.

Cherri Chihuahua was a new student in Essie's class this year. Essie noticed that she liked to do what she wanted to do, when she wanted to do it, instead of following the teacher's directions the first time she heard them. Essie could tell that some changes needed to be made if Cherri was going to do well in 3rd grade. The counselor told

Essie's class that they were the ones who are in control of what they do with their feelings and moods. They are also in control of the choices they make. {Discuss: What do you think the counselor meant?}

Rule #1: You cannot control other people. You can only control yourself.

The teacher told the class to put their white boards in their desks along with some papers that they had been working on. Cherri didn't want to put things away just yet so she kept her group from earning a point by having the their desks cleared first. She began to cry when the other dog members said it was her fault. They were one point away from having a movie at lunch in the classroom with the teacher and they could have had it if she had followed directions.

When the teacher was teaching about making graphs in math, Cherri took out her new markers and admired all the colors instead of listening. Then when the teacher wanted the class to practice using data to make a bar graph, Cherri didn't know what the teacher was talking about. She said it wasn't her fault and began to cry.

"Oh dear," Essie thought. {Discuss: Why would Essie think that?} "Cherri is not taking responsibility and she is not being honest. She's also not showing self control. She should keep her hands out of her desk because our school supplies are not toys."

Later, the other dogs had their own ideas of what they wanted to do at recess. Cherri tried to boss them around and tell them they would be playing a game she made up. They went off and left her by herself. She began to cry again and said it wasn't her fault. She told the teacher the other dogs were being mean and leaving her out. Cherri smiled when the teacher scolded the other dogs. They decided she couldn't be trusted to tell the truth. {Discuss: What do you think of Cherri's ideas for making friends?}

Rule #2: If you want a friend, you need to be a friend.

That evening Cherri told her parents she didn't have any homework, even though she did. She didn't feel like doing it. Remember self-control means you are in charge of you and you need to do things even if you don't necessarily want to. It's not summer vacation and that means homework needs to be done, you need to have a bedtime, and you go to school even if you don't feel like it and would rather stay home and play. {Discuss: What would happen at your

54

house if you weren't being honest about having homework?}

Cherri was into a video game about chasing cats and her parents told her she could play it for as long as she wanted as a reward for doing so well at school. Cherri didn't tell them how it was really going at school and played with her video game until it was time to go to bed. After she got into bed, she sneaked her tablet under the covers and began to play some more. She was almost at the next level and that would mean more shiny tags on a virtual dog collar! Her eyes began to droop from being so tired and even when she finally closed them to go to sleep, she could still see the bright lights in her mind flickering on the screen. {Discuss: Share any rules you have at your house about electronics before bedtime.}

Rule #3: When you prioritize, the important things you have to do get done first. Then you have time for the things that you want to do. "Have to do" comes before "Want to do".

Since it was so late when she went to bed, she had a hard time getting up the next morning. When Cherri got to school, she was a grouchy Chihuahua and showed her teeth and growled at other dogs who were trying to be friendly on the school bus. Her day was not getting off to a good start and as usual, Cherri didn't see how that was her fault. {Discuss: Can you help her figure out how she is in control of her day?}

Rule #4: You have a choice. You can be kind to others or you can be mean. You can look for what you don't

**like about someone or you can find something you like
about the person.**

Essie had seen enough and decided to have a talk with
Cherri.

"Cherri," he said. "You have such a beautiful name.
Besides being somewhat of an expert at self-control, I'm
also pretty good at figuring out what names stand for. Like
mine is Essie, or the letters S C for short, and that stands for
self control. Since it does, it's my honor and duty to show
that I have self-control."

Cherri was listening very closely. "What do you think
my name stands for?" she wanted to know.

"You have some very important words that go with your name. I have figured out that everywhere you go, your name represents our character traits: Caring, Honesty, Empathy, Responsibility, Respect and Integrity. The problem is Cherri, that I don't see you showing those character traits."

Rule #5: Others notice the choices you make. Be sure you are making choices that represent the person you want to be.

Cherri began to feel ashamed because she knew Essie was right. She hadn't been caring or honest or responsible. She didn't show empathy when she got her classmates in trouble and Essie didn't even know about her untruths at home that showed she didn't have integrity or respect for her parents.

"What am I going to do? I've been given a name that requires so much and I haven't been showing those character traits."

"Would you like me to help you, Cherri?" offered Essie. When I see that you are about to do something that is un-Cherri-like, I could give you a signal."

"Like what?" asked Cherri.

"Well, I could jiggle my collar or scratch my ear or….?" {Can you think of some other ways Essie could send a signal to Cherri?}

"Let's try it!" said Cherri. I want to make some changes. I want to be all those things my name stands for. Thank you, Essie."

"Why don't you join the Lightbulb Club? It's a lunch bunch where we talk about things like this and we have loads of fun!" She couldn't wait to sign up.

It wasn't easy but Cherri stopped and thought before she spoke, thought about how what she was about to do would make someone feel, and most importantly, thought about how she was going to feel about herself when she thought about her actions. And do you know? She got an award at the end of the school year character assembly for Integrity! Integrity is like an umbrella for all of the other character words combined. Cherri was so proud of the ribbon she received. And now, even though the assembly is over, Cherri makes the ribbon a part of her outfit every day.

Rule #6: Even if you don't get an award at an assembly, you can create the person you want to become and be proud about it every day!

Activities to accompany "Essie and Cherri Chihuahua"
The story may be used in segments with the group
addressing one part of the story in each session.

Rule #1
Start a tabletop discussion of what students think they have
control over and what they don't. Facilitate the discussion
so they include that their choices about behaviors and
attitudes are what they can control and things they can't
control include the weather, the time, and other people.
Have students complete the Things I Can Control worksheet
in the Supplementary Resources section.

Rule #2
Divide the students into pairs. Students in each pair will
brainstorm together what they have in common and ways
each is different. Have them write each idea they come up
with on a slip of paper. Give each pair two hula hoops (the
P. E. department is a great resource for this). Use them as a
Venn Diagram to compare and contrast similarities and
differences.
Share and discuss. Can we have friends who are different
than we are? How does that make a friendship interesting?

Rule #3

Each student will complete an Electronics Device Profile (in the Supplementary Resources section) and share with each other. Add to the conversation about research that shows that devices should be turned off an hour before bedtime. Why?

Rule #4

The choice is yours. You can either focus on things that you don't like about someone or you can focus on being positive and look for the goodness in others.

Ask group members to remove one shoe and line them up against the wall. These will be their mailboxes. Give students enough strips of paper to write an individual positive message to each group member. Monitor and read what students are writing to ensure their message is positive and appropriate. Students will fold their messages and deliver them to the shoe mailboxes.

Rule #5

Using the letters of your name, can you come up with some ideas that promote good character? Have students decorate their inspiring messages.

For example, **B**e kind to others

Inspire others with your words

Look out for other peoples' feelings

Lend a hand when needed

Rule #6

Make and decorate an award you would like to receive at a character assembly. What would it look like? What would it say? Why would you be receiving the award? What can you do today that will work toward earning the award of your dreams?

Idea: Have paper cutouts available in various shapes for students to use in designing their award.

Implementation Suggestions

The Lightbulb Club uses data to determine who should participate, how each individual student is progressing, and overall effectiveness of student participation. For the most "wattage" from this program, an element of guided practice in the classroom provided by the counselor is included. This puts counselors in the setting where what has been taught in the small group setting is applied into practice. Timely, firsthand, formative data can be collected regarding the application of skills and this data can be used to inform the counselor about next steps. For example, does something you presented need to be retaught to the whole group or differentiated to make more sense to an individual learner? Keep in mind the concepts presented in The Lightbulb Club require time and practice with constructive feedback.

Guidelines are included how to make this hybrid program work. Focus on celebrations and recognize how each student is improving, even if it is a small increment in the right direction. Your data provides the evidence. Be specific in your conversations with individual students when acknowledging incremental steps of improvement so that the student is clear about what they are doing differently that is contributing to making progress toward their goal. For example, "I notice it is helping you pay attention by leaving your toys at home." or "I saw you raising your hand to participate twice when I stopped by your classroom. You were tuned in to your teacher's channel." If students can repeat these practices making them a habit, it should become apparent over time in the quantitative data you collect from future report cards and progress reports.

Enforce the same expectations in the small group setting as what the expectations are for the classroom. This provides alignment and practice in the small group setting. For example, raise hand and wait, one person talks at a time, "catch" directions the first time around, and stay in your invisible bubble (personal space). From time to time during a session, pause, choose a member and ask, "What did I just say?" to see who was really listening versus just hearing your voice. Were they tuned in to your channel or on autopilot?

In each session, create throughout, a positive "You can do it!" atmosphere. This is not punitive work. You are helping students build skills. The underlying belief is that with effort and perseverance, students can change, progress, and achieve greatly.

Let's Look at the Data

Check students' first progress report or report card focusing in on the Work Habits and Conduct sections, or whatever they are categorized as in your district. These are the skills listed on the report card and progress report that include such items as pays attention, follows directions, takes care of personal and school property, adheres to school rules and regulations, exhibits self control, gets along well with others, and shows respect for authority. These are expectations at all levels of education. Students who are earning less than a satisfactory grade in these areas are candidates for The Lightbulb Club. The teacher comment section will give you specifics about areas of improvement needed for the student to maximize potential. This data analysis provides the basis of your Closing the Gap Action Plan.

Throughout the year, you can monitor group members' progress with quarterly progress reports, report cards, and report card comments. If you are including the guided practice component in the classroom, you will have even more data that produces evidence of success as you observe firsthand. A pre/post test is included in the program to be given during the first and last small group sessions to provide more data about the effectiveness of your program.

You may find that you cannot accommodate all of the students at the grade levels who meet the criteria of falling below an S in Work Habits or Conduct. This is where you may cross-reference and prioritize those on your list with those receiving reading services, frequent visitors to the nurse's office, those with office discipline referrals, or some other criteria that pares down your target group of participants.

Getting Started

This program can be used as a stand-alone program or you can supplement it with other materials appropriate for the level you are working with (see ideas below). Blank game cards are included for you to differentiate the games to meet your students' needs. You will base your work upon data to determine group participation (**process data**) and assess the effectiveness of the group work with formative data from report cards, progress reports and the teacher comment section of these documents. You will determine **perception data** when you analyze pre/post test results. Choose an ending data point at the conclusion of your work to determine **outcome data** from report card grades in Work

Habits and Conduct and teacher comments on those report

cards. One plan is to identify students early in the school

year after the first progress report and work with them in

groups until the end of the third quarter. The third quarter

report card is your ending data point to determine outcome

data. Another plan would be shorter in duration, with

members added or dropped based upon quarterly data or the

length of time that works for your school. You will use this

information to create your results report to share with others.

Create a spreadsheet with each member's name listed and

spaces to input their progress in Work Habits, Conduct and

teacher comments that note improvement. This is your

running record throughout the child's participation in the group and will be used to track formative data.

Familiarize yourself with the components of The Lightbulb Club program. Prepare games ahead of time and gather materials so you are ready to begin. If you are going to supplement, start thinking about what games or activity books you already have that address memory building, direction following, and listening. Gather what is appropriate for the age group you are working with. You can include these during your group time. Other ideas include cutting out activities from the kids' section in the newspaper that you may want to use. The party game where several items are on a tray, shown to students for thirty seconds and then writing what they remember is an example of a fun activity you can do with students to help practice focus, memory, and working on a time-sensitive task. Similarly, some icebreakers may give you some ideas. An example is each student taking a turn to introduce him/herself along with an interesting fact to share. Each student in turn must introduce all that have gone before and remember the interesting fact about each person before introducing themselves. Inventory the books you already have and visit your school's library for books that illustrate the importance of following directions, staying in one's personal space, the necessity of attentive listening skills and add these to your resources to use with the group.

A sample parent letter is included which describes The Lightbulb Club and after you have received parent permission, your groups are ready to be formed. If you are pushing-in to provide guided practice, you will want to alternate weeks you have groups, with weeks you will be doing classroom monitoring. The monitoring will focus on the implementation of the skill(s) that has/have been presented thus far during small group work.

Scheduling

Decide how many sessions you want to commit to this. One example is:

2 weeks meet with groups

1 week in classrooms

2 weeks meet with groups

1 week in classrooms

This pattern continues for the duration of your group work.

Another example that has worked well for Lunch Bunches is:

First week: group work for grade level A and push in with grade level B

Next week: group work for grade level B with push in at grade level A

This pattern continues for the duration of the group sessions.

If you are doing Lunch Bunches, plan to pick up students at their classrooms and take them to get their lunches in the cafeteria. It will save time with you directing the group's transition from their classrooms to your office. You will want to plan the session with a counselor-directed activity in the beginning so that students may eat and listen and then as they finish, they can move their trays or lunchboxes to a place in your office that clears the workspace for them.

They like the idea of participating in a working lunch and the teachers and parents appreciate your respecting instructional time by meeting during lunchtime.

Lunchtime can be a teachable moment for the group members depending upon where your office is located. If it is a well-traveled hallway to and from the cafeteria, students can evaluate how well certain classes are observing the expectations for hallway behavior. They can determine whether or not they hear a lot of talking from a class going by or if students are knocking unnecessarily on the door or looking in the window, and give a silent signal with their thumb to other group members to show how well they think the class is doing. Be sure you make the connection that others listen to group members' hallway behavior throughout the day and that self-control equals thumbs-up behavior.

One more note about Lunch Bunches is that they work well because there is no interruption to instructional time and students usually love the special treat of eating in the counselor's office. However, you may not be able to meet with all of the students during that timeframe so an alternative is for teachers to suggest a convenient time for pulling students for group. When teachers see how closely you are working them in support of their instruction, other times may open up. Your work will be seen as very valuable.

Based upon your data at your planned termination point, you may want to end participation for some but continue with others. Your overall review of data via report cards or progress reports at a grade level may inform that someone else needs to be in the group who hasn't been a member previously. Keep using data to drive your work. Monitor anyone who has been dismissed so they may continue participating if they need continued support.

Guided Practice in the Classrooms

Discuss your program with the teachers ahead of time so they will know that when you visit, that you are not there to talk to them and they will continue with the lesson. After you visit a few times, the students will accept your being there without asking why. Visit the classrooms that have students you are working with to provide practical guided practice in the application of the skills. Schedule your time to visit classrooms more than once during the week at various times of the day. Don't forget recess and special classes where self-control may be put to the test.

Inconspicuously sit and watch what students are doing when the teacher is instructing. If you see that one of them is off task requiring redirection, go over and sit by the student and remind him about "tuning in to the teacher's channel". When directions are given, observe what students in your target group are doing. If they have been on "autopilot" and now are jolted back to the lesson with an expected task, go over and sit by them to review the directions to get them back on track.

Create a grid sheet with group members' names and put a check by their name as they are doing what is expected. A student may earn several checks within a visit. If the teacher gives positive feedback regarding a student between group sessions, another check can be earned on the tally sheet for that student. The student with the most checks between group sessions can be recognized the next time the group meets and earn an academic-related prize from the prize box (example: pencil). They will want to be noticed doing what they are expected to do.

An alternative to the grid sheet is taking anecdotal notes and recognizing members the next time you get together for meeting the expectation. Focus on the positive. Addressing the student who is continuing to struggle is best left for a private conversation to provide guidance.

Individually meet with each group member to review their report card to provide feedback. Get the student's feedback of how they think they are doing, too. Their perception may be different than the teacher's. You can prepare a Data Folder for each child. They can file their goal sheet from the first session and subsequent goals that they set to work on based on report cards, progress reports,

teacher comments and your observation.

Suggested Use of the Program Example: Story #1

Session 1: Prepare ahead of time:

*a drawing of a lightbulb on a white board poster with skills

you are going to be focusing on in the group

*Blank copy of report card to show students the sections that

will be the group's focus

*Lightbulb Goal Sheet

     Introductions/ Group Rules/Pre-test

     Students learn about skills listed in the lightbulb and

become familiar with their grade level's report card

     Students write their personal goal in their copy of

Lightbulb Goal Sheet (Supplementary Resources section)

Read the story of "Essie: The Dog Who Learns Self-Control" up to Rule #7 as an overview

Session 2: Re-read the section of the story about Essie up to Rule #1 and discuss

Rule #1 Accompanying Activity

Student recognition

Session 3: Review the story about Essie from previous week and read section for Rule #2

Rule #2 Accompanying Activity

Introduce The Lightbulb Club Game

Student recognition

Session 4: Students retell the story about Essie up to this point. Read section about Rule #3

Rule #3 Accompanying Activity

Play The Lightbulb Club Game

Student recognition

Session 5: Recap prior knowledge about the story about Essie and read section for Rule #4

Activity for Rule #4 (use of magnets)

Introduce The Game of Self Control

Student recognition

Session 6: Group members take turns telling the story up to that point

Read the section pertaining to Rule #5

Activity for Rule #5

Group choice: Play The Game of Self Control or The Lightbulb Club Game or both!

Session 7: Group members retell story

Focus on Rule #6

Activity Rule #6

Play The Game of Self Control or The Lightbulb Club Game

Session 8: Group members tell story up to this point

Focus on Rule #7 and ending of story

Show students the "magic!" with Essie's name (Essie turns in to SC which turns in to the abbreviation for self-control)

Students learn the song about Essie

Post-test

Draw a blank game board on a whiteboard or poster board. Have students fill in the spaces with tips they now know about showing self-control (for example, raise hand and wait to be called on or stay in your own invisible bubble). Use game pieces or magnets on the whiteboard and dice to play.

Celebrations and Closure

Making the Games

The Lightbulb Club Game

The object of this game is bright thinking. The goal is for students to practice catching the directions or responding to the question the first time they hear it. They then use "think time" rather than impulsively responding. The others in the group during this time are listening patiently without making noise. Students who are shouting out that they know the answer, or raising their hands with excited noises, or calling out an answer, are not helpful to the person who is thinking. Point this out. If you want to open the question up after a specified time for the others to answer, then you can tell them when that occurs. The procedure is measured, quiet, and relaxed so that students can experience that environment and all can do their best thinking while practicing skills of self-control.

Questions are included for the game but blank cards are also available for you. You want to ensure that the cards you use are appropriate for the level you are working with.

Directions:

You will need dice to determine progression around the game board.

Draw a large lightbulb on poster board. The outline of the bulb will become the game board. Divide it into game squares. Not every square will have a message.

Create a page of small lightbulbs and cut out. Students earn a lightbulb token if the answer they provide demonstrates clear, bright thinking.

Cut out game card messages and tape to the back of the "Show Off Your Watts" cards you will copy. These cards will be placed in the middle of the game board. Blanks are included to make up your own age appropriate tasks.

Find pictures of different types of lights and cut them out for the game pieces. Give them names like Stewart Stoplight, Spencer Spotlight, Hal Halogen, Sophie Softwhite, Larry Lamp, and Nila Nightlight.

Cut out the encouraging messages which are included to decorate the board.

Laminate all parts of the game and you are ready to go!

Show off your watts!

Show off your watts!

Sherry Hall

Facilitator says: Get up and turn off the light. Then turn the light back on and sit back down.

Facilitator says:
2 8 4
Student repeats what was heard.

Facilitator says:
July February June August
Which is a winter month?

Facilitator says:
78 47 127 67
Which number has 3 digits?

Facilitator says: Shake hands with someone beside you and then count backwards from 5 to 0.	Facilitator says: Stand up, hop on one foot 3 times, turn around, and sit down.
Facilitator: Think of the months of the year that start with the letter J and say them out loud.	Facilitator says: 9 4 3 7 Student repeats what was heard.

Facilitator says:
running   singing
walking   skipping

Which one does not belong?

Facilitator: What word can you make if you put together the second letter of the alphabet and the fifth letter of the alphabet?

Facilitator says:
Look at the clock and tell everyone what time it is. What time will it be an hour from now?

Facilitator says:
How many crayon colors can you name that start with the letter B?

Facilitator says: 127 6 84 Student repeats what was heard.	Facilitator says: football soccer flowers basketball Which one does not belong?
Facilitator says: Touch your nose 3 times with your finger and tap your should twice.	Facilitator spells: t-r-a-i-n What is the second letter I said?

Facilitator says: 75, 74, 73, 72,... What comes next?	Facilitator says: Think of the thing that has 4 wheels, is yellow, and brings children to school. Count how many letters there are in that word. Add one more. What number do you get?
Facilitator says: If Monday is the first day of the school week, what is the fourth day of the school week?	Facilitator says: *On* is the opposite of *off*. *In* is the opposite of *out*. What is the opposite of *dark*?

Facilitator says: You left your lunch on the bus this morning. Come up with 3 ways to solve your problem.	Facilitator: You are late for school many mornings because you are not ready when the bus comes. What could you do to solve your problem?
Facilitator: State everyone's first name going clockwise in the group. Student will state the names in the same order.	Facilitator: Come up with a word that describes you that starts with the first letter of your first name.

Facilitator: To everyone in the group: Count how many letters are in your name and hold up the number with your fingers. To the student: Who has the same amount of letters in their name as you do?	Facilitator: What would you draw so we would know what your favorite season is?
Facilitator: Name 5 kinds of transportation.	Facilitator: Count the number of eyes in the room. How many does it equal?

Sherry Hall

The Lightbulb Club

Glow brightly

Use your good brain

Shine on

Think before you speak

The Lightbulb Game

The Game of Self Control

This game reinforces skills taught in the group by moving forward or backwards on the game board. Cards and game square messages are used as springboards of conversation between the group members.

Directions:

-On a poster board, draw the letter S and connect it to the back of a letter C. Divide the letters into 24 game squares (14 on S and 10 on C).

-Each square will have a task or a "Take a Card" label. Cut out all of the labels and glue them on the game board.

*Note that the students make a choice at the intersection of the S and the C so attach the ←--→ label there. There are two pledge labels for both endings of the letter C.

-Cut out the game card messages and the "Hold On to Your Self Control" cards.

-Tape each message to the back of a "Hold On to Your Self Control" Card.

-Cut out the game tokens.

-Laminate all pieces.

-Gather a koosh ball, dice, a craft stick to attach to a stop sign cut out, and a pinwheel.

For the game board

The Game of

Self-Control

After you draw The SC gameboard, cut and paste these messages in the squares. See game board example.

START

Talk about what you wish a student would stop doing in your class that distracts you. Don't mention any names.

I can feel myself getting ready to pop! Can I take a walk around the

halls with the counselor to cool off instead? What else could I do to turn my angry feelings around?

THINK! Is getting upset about this worth losing my self-control? Talk about a time you let something go and didn't make a big deal out of it.

TAKE A CARD

TAKE A CARD

TAKE A CARD

TAKE A CARD

TAKE A CARD

TAKE A CARD

Use the pinwheel and show the others
how you can calm down by taking a deep
breath in for the count of 4 and
then blowing it out for the count of 4.

_____

To make your hands feel better,
Squeeze the koosh ball tightly for
4 counts and let it go.

_____

Hold up the stop sign. Say "STOP!"
I need to think what will happen
next with the choice I am about to
make. Talk about a time when
you made the better choice.

_____

I will go to a quiet spot in the
classroom to keep in control.
Read the Quiet Corner ideas to the group.

Quiet Corner Activities

1. Close your eyes and get quiet. Open them when you are ready.
2. Write about your feelings.
3. Read or look at pictures in a book.
4. Slow down your breathing. Take a breath in for 4 and blow it out for 4.
5. Show how you're feeling with a drawing. What colors show anger?
6. Squeeze the koosh ball for 4 and relax. Repeat.
7. Massage your own shoulders.
8. Tense up your legs (toes toward your knees). Hold for 4 counts, relax, and then repeat.
9. Give yourself a hug.
10. Think about your favorite things.

Self-control is about making good choices. Choose which way you would like to go next.

TAKE A PLEDGE TO SET THE EXAMPLE AND SHOW OFF YOUR SELF-CONTROL.

Do you think there is a connection
between self-control and grades?
What is it? See how many group
members agree with you.

Who would you like to talk about
(no names) who sets the example
and shows great self-control?
What do they do?

When I walk down the hall, I
keep my hands to myself. I
clasp them behind me if I think
I might forget. I'll show you.
Ask a group member what another
hall rule is.

Think about the job you would
like to have in the future.
Why do workers at that job
have to have self-control?

No one needs to know I am walking
by their room when I am in the hall.
I can put a finger over my mouth
or make my mouth into a bubble
of air if I need to remind me.
I'll show you. Ask a group member
why we should be quiet in the halls.

Think about the job you would
like to have in the future. Why
do workers at that job have to have
self-control?

_____

Who in your family has the most
self-control? What do they do
that makes you think that?
Who do you think in your family
has the least self-control?
What do they do that makes you think that?

_____

Talk about what works for you to tune out people who are distracting you. If you don't have an idea, see if one of the group members does.

Cards to go with The Game of Self Control
These go on the back of the "Hold on to your self control" cards.

We put our feet on the floor under our desk. It is not where we sit and pout. Go back to START.	I raise my hand and wait to be called on before I speak. Move ahead 2 spaces.

I found money that was not mine on the floor while the teacher was teaching so I got up out of my seat and put it in my backpack. What would be a better choice? Go back 3 spaces.	My eyes are on the teacher, I am listening and participating. Move ahead 3 spaces.
We are sitting on the rug listening to a story. I see some fuzz I can play catch with while the teacher is reading. Do you think this is distracting? If so, to who? Move back 1 space.	Tell the other players about a time you showed self control. Go ahead 3 spaces.

When our class is sitting criss-cross applesauce on the rug, I like to hug the person beside me. Am I in my personal space? Go back 2 spaces.	I just thought of something! I brought a toy to school and it is in my backpack. Even though I'm supposed to be doing some work, I'm going to get up right now and go and get it. Go back 3 spaces.
When my teacher says it is time to listen, I stop talking and make eye contact with her, the first time she says it. Go ahead 4 spaces.	I set a good example and I keep my hands to myself. I pretend that each of us has an invisible bubble around us and I respect personal space. Go ahead 5 spaces.
I am quiet in the school hall. I know that others are working and they do not need to know I am passing by. Go ahead 3 spaces.	I just want to turn in my paper when I'm finished and be done with it but I know how important it is to check over my work. Everybody makes mistakes sometimes and I want to make the choice to catch mine while I still have it. Go ahead 5.

Someone told me a rumor about a classmate and wants me to pass it on to another classmate but I am going to make a better choice. I don't choose to be a part of it. Go ahead 3 spaces.	I don't feel like doing my work and nobody can make me. I am choosing to say mean things and now I'm going to throw my shoes at the wall to get everyone's attention. Go back to START.

Hold on to your self-control. Don't give it up!

Hold on to your self-control. Don't give it up!

| Hold on to your self-control. Don't give it up! | Hold on to your self-control. Don't give it up! |

SUPPLEMENTARY RESOURCES

Sample Parent Permission Letter

Dear Parent of _____,

Your child is invited to join a small counseling group called *The Lightbulb Club*, that supports academic success by targeting work habits and conduct. Some work will be done in a small group setting in my office as a "lunch bunch", while other work is done in the child's classroom with my providing guided practice as students apply the skills they are learning.

We will be discussing:

> Awareness of how they are distracting themselves and others
> How to focus and truly listen
> Setting the stage with their bodies that makes listening more likely to
happen
> Developing "blinders" to tune out competing stimuli
> Building thinking stamina
> Tuning into the "teacher's channel"
> Importance of eye contact
> How to get off "autopilot" and mindfully listen
> Why toys and other distractions should be left at home

We will also spend time with:
> Memory Games
> Activities for following directions the first time they are given
> Building listening skills
> Problem solving

Please give your permission by _____ as groups will be starting soon. If you have any questions, please give me a call.

Sincerely,

My child_____has permission
to join *The Lightbulb Club*.

_____   _____

Parent Signature   Date

_____   _____

Teacher's Name   Grade

Name_____

The Lightbulb Club Goal Sheet

Draw a lightbulb and make copies of the goal sheet for students.

Directions: I think I need to work on this to have better days at school. Write your answer in the lightbulb. You can have more than one answer.

Essie, the Dog with Self-Control

(With musical note names)
Sung with a beat

G E
Es-sie,

G   A   A   A   G   E
The dog with self con-trol

Spoken: You can do it!

G E
Es-sie,

G   A   A   A   G   E
He worked to meet his goal

Spoken: Yes, he did it!

C   C   C   C   B   A   G   G
He used to make a lot of noise

A   A   A   G   G   E   E
Both-er-ing the girls and boys

C   C   C   B   A   A   G   G   G   G
Get-ting in their in-vis-i-ble bub-ble

A   A   AA G   G   E   E   E
End-ing up in all kinds of trou-ble

E   G E
Now Es-sie,

G G A   A   A G   E
He's a dog with self con-trol

Spoken: Now he's got it!

G E
Es-sie,

G   A   A   A G   E
He worked to meet his goal

Spoken: Yes, he did it!

C   C   C   C   C B A G   G
Es-sie stops and thinks of a good choice

A A   A   A   A   A G   G G E   E
Sets the ex-am-ple with his bod-y and voice

C   C   C   C   C   B   A   G   G   G
Fol-lows di-rec-tions the first time a-round

A   A   A   A   A   G   G   E   E   E
Shows re-spect in the school, bus and play-ground.

G E
Es-sie,

G G A   A   A G E
He's a dog with self con-trol

Spoken: Now he's got it!

G E
Es-sie,

G   A   A A G   E
He worked to meet his goal

Spoken: Yes, he did it!

Ending spoken: Way to go, Essie!!! (thumbs up)

Which Part of the Brain?

A=Amygdala   H=Hippocampus PFC=Pre Frontal Cortex

Somebody cut ahead of me in the lunch line while I was waiting for my tray so I elbowed them back behind me. A

I remembered to keep the toy I brought for indoor recess in my backpack. Last time I brought a toy and was playing with it when the teacher was teaching and she took the toy and kept it until the end of the day. H

Michelle says things that hurt my feelings so I am going to give her an I-message. I am going to tell her how I feel when she does that and ask her to stop. PFC

I remembered what the counselor said about tattling and reporting so I am not going to tell the teacher that Joey rolled his eyes at me. H

Last time I was in the lunch line, I was goofing around with my friends instead of paying attention. I was embarrassed when I realized I was keeping everyone from getting their food including me, so this time I will take care of business and choose what I want and keep it moving. PFC

Brad got in my personal space so I shoved him out of it. A

My little brother was chasing his ball and was getting close to the busy street so I ran across the grass after him. A

The doorbell rang and when I peeked out the window by the door, I saw two ghosts and ran! A

The doorbell rang and when I peeked out the window by the door, I saw two ghosts and ran but then I looked at the calendar and remembered it was October 31st. H

The doorbell rang and when I peeked out the window by the door, I saw two ghosts and ran but then I looked at the calendar and remembered it was October 31st. Then I went back to the door, opened it up, and heard "Trick or Treat" and gave the ghosts some candy. PFC

Helpful Mistake or Not a Helpful Mistake

The teacher told me to stop talking but I kept talking to my friend anyway.

Last time I hit a classmate because they were bothering me but then I learned I should use my words instead so that's what I did the next time.

I didn't learn my lunch/library/bus number yet and everyday I get fussed at about it for holding up the line.

I brought a toy from home and played with it during Math. The teacher took it away from me. That happened last week, too.

I keep forgetting to bring my homework to school. The counselor told me to put it in my backpack when I finish it and put my backpack by the door. I don't feel like trying that. Oh well.

When the teacher says come to the rug, I make sure I sit by my friend so we can talk and play while the teacher is reading. The teacher has told me to show better self-control but I don't want to.

I didn't come up with the right answer for a math problem so I started over again and tried a different way to solve it. This time I got it!

Today I didn't cry when I came to a word I didn't know when I was reading. I remembered to stretch out the sounds and figured it out all by myself!

We had a fire drill today and this time I tried to be very quiet. I even put my finger over my lips to remind me because last time I was talking.

When I make a mistake, I try another way and if that doesn't work, I try another way. I keep on going until I get it, even if my pencil eraser gets all used up.

I got out of my seat when the bus was moving to hit a 3rd grader I don't like. I got written up and had to go to the principal's office. I'm going to hit his friend when I see them on the bus today.

My teacher heard some friends and me playing in the bathroom and making a mess with the water. We had to help the custodian mop up the floor. I will not spend my time playing in the bathroom again.

My Brilliant Brain Poem

Amygdala, amygdala
Fight, run or freeze
The first thing that I thought of
Let me think a minute, please

Hippocampus, filing cabinet
Memories I save
Everything I've learned or heard
And ways I should behave

Pre-frontal cortex

PFC

Let me stop and think about

A choice so good to shout about

I love my brain!

I love my brain!

Name_____Grade_____ Pre/Post 1

1. What is an invisible bubble?
   a. soapsuds
   b. something made from bubblegum
   c. a way to think about personal space

2. What is one way I can show I am listening?
   a. play with toys in my desk that I brought from home
   b. answer a question the teacher asks
   c. whisper about recess to another classmate

3. What is autopilot?
   a. letting everybody else do the work
   b. using my good brain to think
   c. being a part of the lesson by participating

4. What does it mean to tune in to the teacher's channel?
   a. I catch the directions the first time around and I can tell you what the teacher just said.
   b. I am daydreaming about what I'm doing after school today.
   c. I have my hands in my desk playing with this cool thing I brought from home.

5. I show self-control by
   a. saying naughty words
   b. being in someone else's personal space
   c. raising my hand and waiting until the teacher calls me

Name_____Grade_____Pre/Post 2

1. When my mind is full of what I should be doing or thinking about right now, it is
called_____.

2. When I do the first thing that I think of without stopping and thinking what would be the best choice, I have listened to my:
    a. pre-frontal cortex
    b. hippocampus
    c. amygdala

3. When I stop and think before I act or say something, I am using my:
    a. pre-frontal cortex
    b. hippocampus
    c. amygdala

4. When I remember what happened right after I made a certain choice (for example, I felt good about my choice or I was uncomfortable having a timeout), I am using my:
    a. pre-frontal cortex
    b. hippocampus
    c. amygdala

5. If I want to get better at something,
    a. I can ask for help or try harder
    b. I can blame somebody else for it
    c. I will never get better at whatever it is

Name_____Grade _____Pre/Post 3

1. Having self-control means all of the following except:

    a. I want to do what I want whenever I want.
    b. I stay in my own personal space.
    c. I make good choices about what I say.
    d. I am not playing in my desk when the teacher is teaching.

2. This person is in charge of my choices, my actions, and my attitude.
    a. my Mom
    b. my Dad
    c. me
    d. my teacher

3. Research tells us that to get our best sleep, electronic devices should be turned off how soon before bed?
    a. 1 minute
    b. 1 hour
    c. 4 hours
    d. They should always be turned off.

4. People who use electronic devices right before sleeping:

    a. fall asleep later at night
    b. are sleepy during the day
    c. confuse their brain
    d. all of the above

Name_____'s
My Electronic Device Profile

What devices do you use?

What do you do with the device?

If you could only play one thing, what would be your favorite activity or game to play on your device?

Is homework done before or after you play on your device? Be honest!

Do you play with a device while you eat dinner?

Do you take a device to bed and play before you go to sleep?

Where is your device while you are sleeping?

For fun! Keep a log for a week. How much time did you play on a device? How much time did you play with people (not with a device)?

Write what you can control inside the box below. Write things you cannot control in the space outside the box.

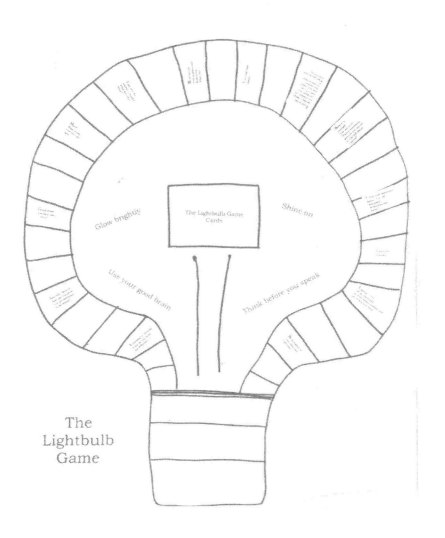

The Lightbulb Game Cards

Glow brightly

Shine on

Use your good brain

Think before you speak

The
Lightbulb
Game

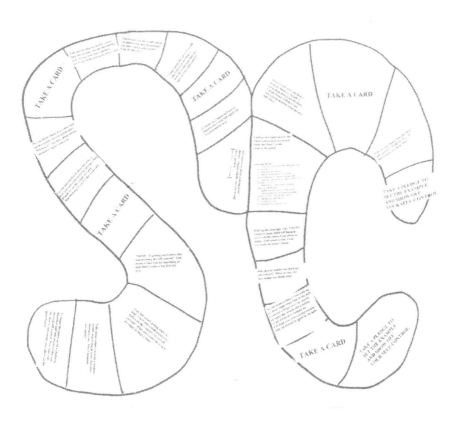

Made in the USA
Charleston, SC
04 August 2016